Essential
Bonsai

Written and designed by Ark Creative • Consultant Editor Jonathan Simpson
Line art illustrations by Edward Baddeley

KUDOS

Published by Kudos, an imprint of Top That! Publishing plc.
Copyright © 2004 Top That! Publishing plc, Tide Mill Way, Woodbridge, Suffolk, IP12 IAP.
www.kudosbooks.com

Kudos is a Trademark of Top That! Publishing plc

Contents

Bonsai Basics

Translated literally, 'bonsai' means 'tree in a pot', but don't be confused into thinking that the term 'bonsai' is exclusive to a particular species of tree. The term applies to the system of growing a happy and healthy miniature tree.

Contrary to popular misunderstanding, bonsai trees are neither stunted nor genetically dwarfed. They are miniature trees or shrubs, nourished, nurtured, then pruned into shape to mimic nature so that the pot and the plant complement one another.

Discovering the art of bonsai will make you see the natural world in a new light. Inspired by nature, bonsai gives you the opportunity to emulate what you see for yourself. Open your eyes to the contorted shapes, twisted forms and aged trunks in the landscape around you.

This book will give you the know-how you need to get started so that bonsai can be your pastime inside or outside – you choose!

The Spirit of Bonsai

Bonsai began as a way of bringing nature into the palaces of Chinese emperors. This turned it into something of a status symbol.

Later, monks of the Chinese Zen religion introduced bonsai to Japan where it was practised as both an aesthetic and a spiritual art form.

The spirit of bonsai is the patient art of practising the embodiment of eternal life.

If you look after your bonsai it will live for a very long time, if not forever! As you begin to care for your plant you will find yourself forming a bond with a living art form.

Just as a tree depends on its roots and on the climate to nurture its growth, so your tree in a pot needs you to nurture it – the life of your bonsai is in your hands.

Buying a Bonsai

Shop around before you buy your bonsai and don't be tempted to buy the first one you like the look of.

Specialist Nursery

Try to locate a specialist nursery where staff are knowledgeable and can share their expertise and plant advice with you. You'll probably find it well equipped with bonsai tools and pots, and it's bound to inspire you to make return trips to see the plants on show and ask for after sales advice.

Main Street

At Christmas watch out for 'bargains' recently shipped in from the Far East and displayed in your main street store. It's very likely that the plants will not be properly looked after once on display so you take the risk of buying a plant of inferior quality.

Mail Order

What you see is what you get! If you're happy to start your new hobby by buying a plant you haven't had the chance to see, touch and get acquainted with, don't be disappointed if it lets you down.

Tips and Hints

Run this health check before you buy your bonsai.

Bottoms Up

Rock the trunk GENTLY and if it rocks easily this may mean the roots are not filling the pot which could signify rot or poor growth.

Mellow Yellow

Yellow leaves are a sure sign of your tree being deficient in either light, water or food – you'd be wise to select a better specimen!

Neat and Trim

Never buy an unpruned tree – it it's well pruned it has been looked after.

Branching Out

Steer clear if you notice a dead branch. It could signify disease, or it could mean that the plant has not been cared for properly.

I Spy Dry

Dry leaves could be down to draughty conditions, a lack of water or a plant pest – watch out for withering which is also an unhealthy sign.

Lush and Leafy
Do not buy a plant with discoloured or distorted leaves – look for a happy plant before you buy.

Bonsai Inside

Now you know what to look for in a healthy plant, it's worth considering where you want to put it so that you can make sure you buy the right plant for the right place. Follow these simple dos and don'ts that will help your bonsai to settle in.

Dos

- Do keep your bonsai out of direct sunlight and hot sun.

- Do keep your bonsai near a west-or east-facing window, or a south-facing window with shade.

Don'ts

- Don't leave your bonsai on the window sill at night where the room temperature may fluctuate.

 For best results, never position your bonsai on a north-facing window, and always take it off the window sill and bring it into the house when you draw the curtains at night.

Bonsai Outside

If you have a garden, you may prefer to cultivate an outside bonsai. Again, follow these simple dos and don'ts that will help your bonsai to settle in.

Dos

- Do position your bonsai in dappled shade and indirect sunlight.

- Do shelter your bonsai from exposed areas.

Don'ts

- Don't leave your bonsai in full sun as the pot will dry out.

Position your bonsai outside in a Japanese pagoda constructed from slatted wood. This is best for your bonsai (because it gives good shelter and dappled shade), and it's best for you (because it looks good and will add an authentic Japanese feel to your garden).

Pick your Pot

You need to select a pot which is in proportion to your bonsai and one which is a size and colour to complement the shape and style of your bonsai.

- Cascading styles should be planted in tall pots (ideally no more than two-thirds of the height and length of the tree) to keep the branches cascading over the top and off the ground.

- Forest groups look best in shallow oval or rectangular pots.

- Set the scene for tall rugged pines in round pots.

- Rectangular pots complement the depth of a conifer with a thick, gnarled trunk or the wide leaves of an evergreen.

- Slim trunks and group plantings look good in shallow pots.

- Wide, spreading styles suit pots that flair out at the top or that are rimmed.

- You'll notice that bonsai pots are not overly decorative – this is so that they do not detract from the pleasing composition of your tree in its pot.

 Always make sure your pot has generous drainage holes, small feet and a level base. You want to ensure that the roots are ALWAYS kept moist.

Select your Soil

You need to ensure that the soil you plant your bonsai in provides it with adequate life support – standard potting compost will not do because it will soon become waterlogged in a shallow pot. Your bonsai needs good drainage, moisture and air to breathe.

As a bonsai beginner, it's best to stick to one kind of soil so that you get used to how to use it. There are various soil types available including clay, 'Akadama' and a mixture of peat and grit.

Clay soil retains the moisture and fertiliser-rich nutrients that you put in it, and is much cheaper than Akadama soil.

Akadama soil (Japanese clay granules) is the preferred soil for specialist bonsai growers because it needs expert handling. It is not recommended for beginners because it contains no nutrients and therefore has no buffer to tolerate any mistakes.

A peat/grit mixture is halfway between Akadama

and clay, and is therefore highly recommended. Mix 1/4 fine grit with 3/4 peat, or 1/2 peat and 1/2 sharp sand.

When replanting always replant your tree into the same type of soil – do NOT switch soils.

Back to its Roots

i. Look underneath the pot for wires coming out of the bottom. This indicates supporting wire. Cut all wire coming out of the bottom mesh and take the tree gently out of its pot. Tease out the long roots so that you can trim them back.

ii. Cut all long, thick roots back to the main root ball. Then trim about a third from the root ball itself.

iii. Cover the drainage holes in the pot (this is to prevent the soil from falling through) using a bonsai gauze/plastic mesh that won't rot or rust and secure in place using plastic-coated wire.

iii.

iv.

iv. Put a very thin layer of soil in the bottom of the pot to replace the soil you have removed so that the bonsai is at its original level in the pot.

Next, gradually add more soil and position the tree reinstating your supporting wire.

v. Finally add the rest of the soil.

vi. Water using a fine spray watering can. Leave to drain.

Replant acers every year to reduce the possibility of acer virus.

Watering Wisdom

Do not use softened water as this builds up salts which could kill your bonsai!

Rainwater
Rainwater is best because it is free of toxins. Collect it in a rain barrel that you keep clean and free of potentially fatal fungi. To do this, put a lid on the top and a tap on the bottom – that way you're not interfering with the tank at all and the water will stay pure.

Tap Water
Filter tap water to rid it of chemicals and let it stand for two hours before watering. This relieves it of chlorine.

Immersion Watering
Place the bonsai in a bowl and slowly cover it with water until you notice air bubbles rising from the soil. Take the bonsai out when you see the bubbles stop, and drain off excess water.

 Immersion watering is the best method because it ensures that the root ball has a proper drink. Make sure the whole root ball is immersed at least 5 mm up the stem.

Fertiliser Facts

Improve your bonsai's diet with the help of some fertiliser, rich in the three main plant nutrients – nitrogen, phosphorus and potassium. It should also contain trace elements such as zinc and magnesium to ensure a proper balanced diet.

- Nitrogen ensures healthy leaves and strong stems
- Phosphates ensure healthy roots
- Potash promotes healthy flowers and builds up the plant's immune system to toughen it up against harsh environmental conditions

Use specialist bonsai fertiliser only!

Remember that the purpose of adding fertiliser is to ensure survival of your bonsai rather than to promote rapid growth so a slow acting fertiliser is best. Steer clear of high doses of nitrogen that will make the leaves extra large.

 Buy a designated bonsai fertiliser and ALWAYS follow manufacturers' instructions.

Start Simple

Use the plant directory to help you choose your bonsai – a Chinese elm likes being inside and outside.

Plant name: Chinese elm *Ulmus parvifolia*

Description: Hardy and prolific. Responds well to pruning and wiring.

Ideal position: Indirect sunlight all year round. Keep in an unheated room in winter, close to a sunny window.

Watering: Keep moist in summer and drier in winter.

Feeding: Feed with a fertiliser every two weeks during the growing season.

Pruning: Prune unwanted branches in early spring, hard prune weak branches in midsummer.

Bonsai style: All styles are suitable, especially informal upright and root over rock.

Pest alert! It may fall prey to spider mites if kept in a warm room in winter.

Chinese elm is a good tree for beginners.

Plants for Inside

Here are some good bonsai for inside.

Plant name: Chinese yew or Buddhist pine *Podocarpus macrophyllus*

Description: Sun loving with evergreen glossy foliage that lasts for several years. Looks very oriental.

Ideal position: In indirect sunlight. Can tolerate a heated room in winter.

Watering: Water regularly in the growing season, spray foliage regularly.

Feeding: The tree will keep growing in winter if you keep it warm.

Pruning: Leaf prune anytime during the growing season.

Bonsai style: Suits all styles except broom. Popular styles include upright and cascade.

Pest alert! Your Chinese yew should stay pest free.

 Roots are very sensitive so root prune very lightly every 2 to 3 years.

Plant name: Olive
Olea europaea
Description: Evergreen, will develop a gnarled trunk as it ages.

Ideal position: Full sun, and moved outside during summer months on to a balcony or into the garden. In autumn bring it inside and position in a cool room.

Watering: Water when the soil surface has dried out slightly as olives are used to a Mediterranean climate.

Feeding: Feed every two weeks in the growing season.

Pruning: Leaf prune early fall or early spring.

Bonsai style: Suits broom and upright best.

Pest alert! Watch out for signs of deformed leaves – a sure indicator of spider mite. This can be fatal to your olive tree if not treated early.

 Prune your olive tree into shape as the brittle branches are not suited to wiring and may snap.

Plant name: Pistachio or Mastic tree
Pistacia lenticus

Description: Evergreen, native of the Mediterranean, with thick glossy leaves growing in all directions.

Ideal position: In indirect sunlight.

Watering: Make sure the soil is kept moist during the growing season.

Feeding: Once a week in the growing season.

Pruning: Prune any time of year.

Bonsai style: Suits broom and informal.

Pest alert! Look out for scale insects.

Help keep your pistachio roots damp by covering the soil surface with moss or gravel.

Plant name:
Tree of a Thousand Stars
Serissa foetida

Description: Small glossy leaves, a gnarled bark and a tendency to a profusion of tiny, white flowers at any time of year make this one of the most popular bonsai trees. It grows fast so you can have fun practising your technique on it.

Ideal position: Indirect sunlight. It needs a minimum temperature of 10 degrees Celsius to stop it from losing its leaves (keep it below 5 degrees Celsius and you'll kill it).

Watering: Serissas thrive if they are kept moist under humid conditions. Spray often with tepid water.

Feeding: Once a week in the growing season.

Pruning: Leaf prune with nail scissors.

Bonsai style: Suits all styles.

Pest alert! None in particular so just stay alert.

 Do not drown the flowers when watering – dry flowers last longer.

Plant name: Sageretia *Sageretia thea*

Description: Evergreen shrub that produces clusters of white flowers. Originally from China, you'll notice it has an intriguing trunk because the bark peels off creating a patchy effect.

Ideal position: Shade loving plant both inside and out.

Watering: Keep well watered during the growing season but ease off in winter. Do not spray the foliage.

Feeding: Feed every two weeks during the growing season.

Pruning: Stem prune in mid winter. You will need sharp tools because the wood is very hard.

Bonsai style: Suits all styles.

Pest alert! Watch out for whitefly.

 Wire training must be done when the branches are young and thin. Old branches break easily.

Plant name: Fig
Ficus

Description: A relation of the rubber plant, all figs produce aerial roots so that their branches are outstretched. Its thick roots will join together which add to its interesting shape.

Ideal position: Likes to sit inside in a warm spot where it can bask in indirect sunlight.

Watering: Water well during the growing season, keep reasonably moist in winter.

Feeding: During the growing season.

Pruning: Leaf prune lightly during the growing season, branch prune in winter to reduce sap.

Bonsai style: Suits all styles.

Pest alert! It is susceptible to scale insect infestation.

 The branches stay flexible for a long time so that you can wire train them. Take care because they thicken quickly. You may need to remove the wire after 6-8 weeks so that it can grow unrestricted.

Plant name:
Japanese privet
Ligustrum japonicum

Description: Evergreen shrub from Japan. It has broad leaves on smooth branches. The black berries that grow from the white flowers are poisonous.

Ideal position: Indirect sunlight, and is happy to be put outside during the growing season.

Watering:
Keep fairly moist.

Feeding: Every two weeks during the growing season.

Pruning: Cut back new growth to between one and five leaf pairs.

Bonsai style: Broom is a good style for this tree.

Pest alert! Watch out for black spot – if you see a light infection remove the infected leaves, if the infection is heavy, spray with fungicide.

 Japanese privet can easily be propagated from cuttings.

Plants for Outside

Here are some good bonsai for outside.

Plant name:
Chinese juniper
Juniperus chinensis

Description: A tough tree, native of the Japanese mountains with prickly foliage, twisted trunk and contorted branches.

Ideal position: Indirect sunlight.

Watering: Water well during the growing season and keep moist in winter.

Feeding: During the growing season.

Pruning: Branch prune in late summer so that the wounds can heal before winter.

Bonsai style: Excellent for all styles.

Pest alert! Red spider mite can be devastating. Regularly check in the leaf axles where they breed – be very vigilant!

A good tree for beginners. Root prune lightly – it could die from heavy root pruning.

Golden juniper shown

Plant name:
Evergreen honeysuckle
Lonicera nitida baggesens gold

Description: Native to China, this is a shrubby honeysuckle with glossy dark green leaves. It is used for hedging as well as bonsai.

Ideal position: Full sun, protected against frost.

Watering: Water well during the growing season.

Feeding: Feed every two weeks during the growing season.

Pruning: Regular trimming will encourage growth and thin out the foliage.

Bonsai style: Suits most styles except broom.

Pest alert! Trouble free.

 Try out some mini topiary on your leafy lonicera and use it as a backdrop to your other bonsai trees.

Acers

(Japanese Maples) are the most popular bonsai with experts and in their native Japan.

Plant name:
Japanese maple
Acer palmatum

Description: Hardy compact tree. The five-lobed palm-like leaves can be bronze in spring, turning from green to a deep red and gold in autumn.

Ideal position: Outdoors, semi shade in summer. Protect from frost and wind.

Watering: Make sure soil is always moist and spray the leaves regularly.

Feeding: Once a week during the growing season – from first extended leaf to autumn colour.

Pruning:
Prune in the spring.

Bonsai style: Suits all styles.

Pest alert! Wind can damage the leaves. Look out for aphids, black fly, white fly, red spider, acer virus.

Plant in groups to highlight the kaleidoscope of natural colors.

Cork bark maple shown

Plant name:
Japanese red maple
Acer palmatum deshojo

Description: A less vigorous variety of maple. One that will reward you with ruby red leaves in spring and in autumn, set against a pale grey bark.

Ideal position: Outdoors, protected from scorching sun or damaging wind. Keep the tree shaded from the afternoon sun.

Watering: Make sure soil is always moist and spray the leaves regularly.

Feeding: Once a week during the growing season – from first extended leaf to autumn colour.

Pruning: Prune in the spring. Trim away crowded branches or twigs.

Bonsai style: All styles, informal upright is popular with the Japanese.

Pest alert! Watch out for aphids, black fly, white fly, red spider, acer virus.

 Acers are best kept in sheltered, dappled shade and are, therefore, ideal for a slatted gazebo.

Plant name:
Kiyohime maple
Acer palmatum kiyohime

Description: A rare, more compact variety of maple with green leaves. It will grow very slowly and is half hardy so needs more care than the other maples.

Ideal position: Outside but protected from any signs of frost. Protect from scorching sun or damaging wind.

Watering: Make sure soil is always moist – spray the leaves regularly.

Feeding: Once a week during the growing season – from first extended leaf to autumn colour.

Pruning: Prune in the spring. Trim away crowded branches or twigs.

Bonsai style: Broom is best.

Pest alert! Watch out for aphids, black fly, white fly, red spider, acer virus.

 This rare maple is more expensive than the common varieties. It is also slow growing and recovers slowly from setbacks.

Plant name:
Mugo pine medium
Pinus mugo 'valley cushion'

Description: Dwarf evergreen with dark green needles on upright branches throughout the year. This is a slow and flat-growing tree hence its name 'valley cushion'.

Ideal position: In dappled shade.

Watering: Keep moist during the growing season and slightly dry in winter.

Feeding: Feed once every two weeks during the growing season.

Pruning: Root prune in early spring. Pinch candles out after the last needle has opened to desired length, and in late autumn prune the branches to required effect.

Bonsai style: Excellent for windswept, raft and cascade.

Pest alert! Watch out for needle scale.

You will find this a flexible tree for wiring into shape. Only root prune conifers every two to three years.

Plant name: Spruce
Picea

Description: Has needle-like leaves shorter than pine and flaking bark which make it an attractive subject for bonsai.

Ideal position: Outside in dappled shade.

Watering: Keep moist during growing season and slightly dry in winter.

Feeding: Feed every two weeks during the growing season.

Pruning: Spruce needs to be pinched (pinch the candles out when they are fully extended) rather than trimmed, and this is best done several times during the spring.

Bonsai style: Forest, upright, but not cascade.

Pest alert! Seek out red spider mites with the aid of a magnifying glass.

 Keep most of the winter rainfall off the root or the roots will get too wet making them prone to root rot.

Dwarf spruce forest shown

Plant name: Japanese yew
Taxus cuspidata

Description: This is an evergreen, slow growing tree with small dark needles. It is also poisonous.

Ideal position:
A shade loving tree.

Watering:
Do not over water.

Feeding: Feed every two weeks during the growing season.

Pruning: Pinch out in spring and as new shoots grow.

Bonsai style: Upright.

Pest alert! Watch out for red spider mite and wooly aphids that attack conifers.

盆栽 You will find this tree easy to style and will be rewarded with the effect of the lush green foliage on gnarled bark.

Plant name: Gingko
Gingko biloba

Description: The oldest of all living trees, sometimes called the 'fossil tree'. Gingko is related to the fern family, so called because 'gingko' (literal meaning 'silver apricot') has seeds that resemble a small apricot, and 'biloba' (literal meaning 'two lobed') because the fan shaped leaves split in the middle.

Be extra vigilant for signs of pests because gingko do not regenerate quickly. Be cautious also not to leaf prune too heavily.

Ideal position: Dappled shade.

Watering: Water and spray foliage regularly during the growing season.

Feeding: During the growing season.

Pruning: Branch prune new branches back to 2–3 buds while the tree is young, during the growing season.

Bonsai style: Informal upright and broom are good styles.

Pest alert! Gingko are very susceptible to all pests.

Ancient to Modern

In ancient China, early bonsai were trained to represent birds and animals – the mythological landscape of dragons and serpents being more highly prized than images of trees. These trees were known as 'pun-sai' – from which the Japanese word 'bonsai' stems.

In Victorian times, travellers returning from the Orient were perplexed to describe tales of strange dwarfed trees, contrived, contorted, and styled to shape. It was not until 1878 when bonsai were displayed in Paris that bonsai became recognised in Europe, as an art form in its own right. In 1909 the garden-loving English later welcomed bonsai as another string to their horticultural bow.

Servicemen returning from Japan in the Second World War brought bonsai back as souvenirs, and after the War, US occupational forces in Japan requested bonsai classes. In 1976 the Japanese presented a bicentennial gift of bonsai to the US which inspired the National Bonsai and

Penjing Museum in Washington, DC.

Today, bonsai can be seen to bridge international friendship and peace!

Traditional Japanese Styles

In your boxed set you will find some wire, a pot, some clippers and a sculpture. These have been specially selected to help you get started on what we are certain will be a bonsai journey without end!

The Japanese devised a selection of styles for bonsai and named them to categorise their form. The names will help you remember the natural effect you are trying to capture as you look at all trees in a different light.

There are two groups of Japanese bonsai styles – 'single trees' and 'forest groups'. Single trees are exactly that, while forest groups are planted to represent nature on a grand scale. You can experiment with different species of tree which will help to obtain a contrast.

Flick through the gallery illustrated in this book and select a style you like.

Top Six

We've selected a 'Top Six' of the most popular single tree styles. These will inspire you to create some variations for yourself. Before you start, here are some tips to help your bonsai stay healthy.

- Do not feed bonsai in winter – they are dormant.

- All bonsai root balls need protecting from frost.

- Position bonsai in dappled shade (outside) and indirect sunlight (inside).

- Always remove and burn all detritus from your bonsai.

- Use moss to cover the root ball – it makes an excellent indicator of the health of your tree. As long as the moss looks healthy, your bonsai should be too!

And finally, remember that all bonsai have quirks and variables according to their species – check with the nursery for special advice on your particular species of tree.

Formal Upright

Chokkan

This is a much sought after style but can be quite hard to achieve. The tree is straight. The branches should alternate at right angles from left to right so that the branches become progressively smaller and it forms a symmetrical pyramid.

This pyramid shape is characteristic of giant conifer trees.

Informal Upright

Moyogi

This style has a gentle, curving trunk, its treetop rising almost centrally above its base. The branches should alternate from side to side and, unlike the formal style, they should start on the outside of a bend.

The main branch gives the tree perspective and the curving trunk should be from side to side (rather than from front to back) which enables you to see the free-flowing movement of the trunk.

There are numerous natural examples created by the harsh effects of the elements.

Cascade

Kengai

This style is representative of a tree in its natural environment, hanging from a cliff or mountain. For this reason it is always planted in tall containers so that the branches overhang.

The thick trunk curves and tapers down, and the branches alternate from side to side. One branch splits and goes down.

Semi Cascade

Han-Kengai

You can differentiate this style from the cascading because although it still appears to be growing down from a cliff, the overall effect is more horizontal.

The branches tend to grow so that one branch grows down and one branch grows up. Planted in a good square pot (not as tall as a cascade pot) this style represents a tree jutting out over a cliff, a river or a lake.

Slanting

Shakan

As a tree is weathered, harsh winds sometimes cause it to blow over leaning sharply to the left or right. Adjusting to its new position exposes the roots so that they look unstable, but remain solid.

To create this effect, plant the bonsai off centre in your pot and style the branches so that they are fairly uniform in position on opposites sides of the trunk.

Broom

Hokidachi

Broom makes a good starting design for beginners because it's quite easy to grow and is one you will be familiar with in nature.

The style is characterised by a straight trunk that divides and sub divides into lots of branches, leading up into an evenly balanced treetop, to give it a broom-like appearance.

Chinese elm is a good plant to start with.

Wired for Style

Wiring is the technique you will use to train your tree into the style you want. The wire holds the branches in place until they set into position. Once set, you can remove the wire and set the branch free. To avoid wire scorch release the wire every three months and reapply as necessary.

To remove the wire from the tree it is best to cut it into small pieces first and then unwind it. This will avoid damage to the bark as it pulls away from the tree.

iii.

iv.

You should not need to keep your tree permanently wired because this will detract from the simplicity of its natural structure and will give it wire scorch. In severe cases where the bark has grown over the wire you will have to leave the wire in place.

Remember that the pressure on the bark increases as the branch thickens. Check often to make sure that the wire does not bite into the bark and if it does, remove it immediately so that you do not scar your bonsai.

Spiralling to Shape

Bond with your tree as you bend its branches. Wire spiralling in order to bend your tree to shape takes time and you will need to listen to your tree to know when to stop. If you hear any cracks you will have to stop and return to wire a bit more some weeks later.

• Cut a piece of wire that is one and a half times longer than the branch.

• Secure it by spiralling it firmly around the trunk or branches.

• Do not spiral in leaves or needles.

• Bend the branches into the direction you want.

• Train the wire to the tip of the branch and bend it round to support the tip of the branch and to ensure a neat bonsai shape.

There are different thicknesses of wire available. Choose the correct thickness of wire to match the branch – both should have the same resistance to bending.

78

Pinching Out

Pinching is an essential part of the conifer pruning process. The needles of your tree will depend on you for this!

The technique allows you to nip out the growth at your desired level to bulk up the plates on the conifer. Pinching out also encourages dwarfing of the new needles, helps to keep the tree compact and encourages open space between the branches which is a very important feature of bonsai.

The photographs show finger pinching the shoots from a Juniper blaauws so that it stays in shape. The shoot should come away with a gentle pinch of your fingers and this is only done on very new fresh growth. Do not use scissors as they make foliage go brown on the tips and they are not as sensitive as your fingers.

i.

 Methods differ depending on whether or not you have chosen a deciduous or a conifer bonsai. Always clear up the leaves you have pruned because decomposing leaves encourage fungal diseases.

ii.

Neat and Trim

Trimming is a pruning technique that will help you maintain your bonsai to the style you like.

Leaf pruning
This is done on deciduous trees during the growing season. Use leaf pruners to cut your tree back to its desired height, taking care to cut just above the leaf joint or node. On most bonsai this is done when the growth is 7–8 cm.

Branch pruning
Used to remove diseased or unwanted branches.

i. Prune in spring when your tree is growing and will heal quickly.

ii. Cut the branch as close to the trunk as possible taking care not to cut into the circular guard cells.

iii. Use a pair of knob cutters and squeeze.

iv. Nurse the wound by sealing it with some pruning compound.

Tools you Need

As your experience grows you can add to your tool kit but the basics included in this boxed set will get you started.

Scissors or garden secateurs (large and small)
For trimming small branches and roots.

Branch or angle branch cutters
To thin out main branches.

Knob cutters
Special tool designed to prune branches without harming the tree.

Leaf pruners
To trim out small stems and leaves.

Rake or root hook
Invaluable when teasing out the root ball before replanting.

Wire cutters
For spiralling and wiring to style.

Coconut brush
To tidy the soil around the base of your tree.

Metal scoop
For pouring the soil into small areas.

Tweezers
Use these if you have sensitive fingertips when pinching out.

Bonsai saw
To remove thick and heavy branches.

Jin brush
To clean up jins.

Shari chisels
To score out the stem and give it a lightning strike.

Bonsai mesh
For drainage in your pot.

Pest Control

The regular watering you give your bonsai will, unfortunately, benefit some common pests. Look on the bright side – your careful bonsai health checks should ensure that you will spot them early!

Aphids (greenflies)
Symptom:
These tiny insects are mainly found on the tips of new growth. They multiply quickly to form clusters that will cover your tree and suck the sap away making it weak. Aphids also attract ants and make the plant susceptible to fungal disease.

Cure:
Spray with suitable insecticide. The 'wooly aphid' (so called because it wears a white fur coat to protect it from insecticide), can be controlled by painting the wooly aphid with methylated spirit. You can also use a systemic pesticide.

Caterpillars

Symptom:
Caterpillars love to feast on foliage and will strip your tree if you let them.

Cure:
Use insecticide powder which stays on the leaves longer and will be munched unsuspectingly by a hungry caterpillar. It is advisable also to under spray the foliage with a pyrethrum spray.

Red spider mite

Symptom:

Unfortunately an attack differs with each bonsai species. Microscopic and barely visible despite their bright colour, red spider mites pierce the backs of the leaves to suck out the sap. You will notice that the leaves of your bonsai appear to be blotchy and yellow.

They are especially partial to conifers causing their needles to turn yellow and brown.

Cure:

Use a pyrethrum based insecticide – repeat application is required once a week.

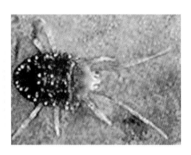

 Heavy misting can reduce an attack because spider mites have difficulty moving when they are wet. Ask your bonsai nursery for an 'acaricide' – the chemical that kills red spider because it will also destroy the eggs.

Scale insects
Symptom:
Scale insects are tiny creatures protected by a scaly outer shell. They cling to the underside of the leaf in order to suck the sap dry. They also encourage the spread of fungal disease.

Cure:
Treat with a systemic insecticide.

Slugs and snails:

Symptom:

Watch out for these sliding up to your tree in the dead of night especially if you are cultivating outdoor bonsai. Slippery trails and lacy leaves are evidence that they are feasting on your tree.

Cure:

Smooth a layer of petroleum jelly around the top of the bonsai pot – making a slippery surface hard for slugs and snails to grip. Pick them off the plant by torchlight at night, and out from convenient hiding places such as underneath the pot where they lurk during the day.

Vine weevil
Symptom:
These white grubs, shaped like half moons are about 5 mm long. They resemble white pearls in the soil and tend to lay their eggs in the compost.
(Adult weevil shown below)

Cure:
Seek expert advice on using a suitable chemical drench.

White fly
Symptom:
Your bonsai will be playing host to a cloud of white insects.

Cure:
Treat with a suitable insecticide.

Common Diseases

To protect your bonsai from disease follow these five simple steps to keep your tree happy and healthy.

• Make sure it is well watered.

• Make sure it gets enough light.

• Make sure it is adequately fed.

• Don't keep unsuitable species inside.

• Make sure it is properly trimmed.

 Always sterilise secateurs after use to protect against acer virus and to control aphids which transmit it.

Acer Virus

Symptom:

This is transmitted by aphids and by using dirty secateurs. The branches wilt at the top and the wilt moves down as the virus progresses – starting on one stem and moving down. Then you will notice black lesions on the stems.

Cure:

You need to completely prune out the infected branch, then isolate the tree in order to stem the further spread of it. Burn ALL infected material.

Black spot
Symptom:
Black spot is a fungal infection that attacks the leaves.

Cure:
Use a general fungicide as a preventative measure and if the attack is mild, remove infected leaves.

Mildew
Symptom:
Mildew masks the leaves in a white, floury layer which will spread over the shoots and leaves. It is sometimes caused by wet foliage, and is a fungal condition that thrives in humidity and poor ventilation.

Mildew is a symptom of a stressed bonsai and often appears after the tree has been water stressed.

Cure:
Spray with a systemic fungicide as soon as you notice white patches appearing on the leaves.

Rust
Symptom:
Rust is also a common fungal disease and occurs in the form of orange or brown blisters spreading over the underside of the leaves. This will cause the leaves to curl up and drop.

Rust is also a symptom of a stressed bonsai.

Cure:
Remove all infected leaves and burn them for a mild attack. Use a copper-based fungicide as a preventative measure to prevent reinfection.

Scab

Symptom:

Scab is a bacteria more often seen on fruit trees and can be caused by a fertiliser over rich in nitrogen. You will notice a shrinking area of the bark that appears to be dry.

Cure:

Cut it out completely to the new wood and make a shari – then coat with vitamin C solution.

Aspiring Styles

Mastering some of the simple styles is an art that will take time. Discover some more styles (single tree and groups of trees) that you may like to strive for later as your confidence in cultivating your bonsai grows.

Rock Landscape

This tree or group of trees is planted on a rock and positioned in a shallow, ceramic dish of water. To achieve this effect you will need to secure the roots in place with wire and secure the tree with sticky compost.

You can use moss on top of the compost to disguise the root ball.

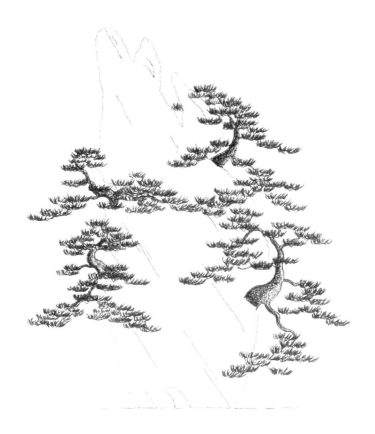

Windswept

Fukinagashi

This impressive style perfectly replicates the natural effects of a windswept tree growing in an exposed place. You may have seen them perched on cliff tops, rooted on moors and isolated on windswept beaches.

The branches are grown all over the tree but you can use the wire to train them in one direction in a horizontal line.

Driftwood

Bankan

This style will take you right back to the roots of bonsai! It is meant to emulate an ancient tree, the trunk curved, twisted and knotted with lots of dead wood as though it has survived lightning and storm damage from many centuries.

You can achieve this by creating your own dead wood. Carefully peel away some of the bark with a chisel – always making sure that some veins of bark

stay intact to provide sap to the living branches.

If you don't feel confident enough to do this, you could attach your tree to a piece of dead wood so that it looks like it is part of the original tree in what is called a 'phoenix graft'.

Literati

Bunjingi

Mirroring the ancient art of calligraphy, this style has an elegant form with a slightly slanting trunk, its branches and foliage developing only at the top.

It is usually tall and thin with very few branches resembling an old pine tree on the horizon. The branches (three only are needed) usually grow down towards the bonsai container so that your eye is trained to see the shape as though it is the downward flourish of the calligrapher's pen.

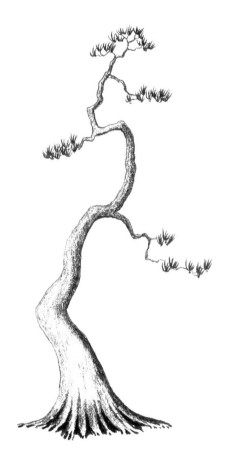

Root over Rock

Ishitzuki

This is a very specific form for plants grown on, or in, the crevices of rocks or boulders. The exposed roots must clasp onto a rock before adding soil into the pot.

The top is exposed gradually to reveal the roots and rock, while the deep roots enable it to feed from the soil.

Raft

Ikada Buki

This is a clever optical illusion where the trunk of a single tree lies just below the soil surface. Planted on its side the branches rise vertically giving the illusion of a group of trees planted side by side.

This is a good style to try if you have a damaged tree trunk because this way you can hide it. Remove small squares of bark

from the underneath of the trunk to help initiate roots all the way along.

Raft is always planted in long, thin rectangular pots and the biggest branch is in the near centre of the pot.

Clump

Sankan

This style represents several trunks coming from the same point at the base of a single tree. It is important to make sure that the trunks are not identical in size because they represent a family.

The two larger trunks are the mother and father, the smaller trunk is the son.

Forest Group

Yose Ue

This is usually planted in a flat and shallow oval or rectangular pot. Alternatively it could be planted on a moss-covered stone base.

The forest group resembles a miniature forest, with different sizes of tree. The tallest tree with the thickest trunk will be at the front, the thinner ones will be behind and the shorter ones to the side. The trees might be positioned in two groups with a space between.

The single trees should have varying space between them.

Setting the Scene

We've given you a Chinese sculpture to complement your bonsai, and to help you create a true bonsai landscape of your own.

The creative potential for making a miniature landscape of your own is limitless! Traditionally, at special times of the year, the Japanese elite bring their bonsai inside for display on a 'tokonoma'. The tokonoma is a special display area in every Japanese home, used to show off ornaments and prized possessions.

Why not set the scene yourself by introducing some figurines for true authentic display? There is a wide variety of ornaments available including pagodas, wise men, bridges, stones and boats.

These will further embellish the landscape and, traditionally, are meant to ward off evil and bad spirits!

Display Away

How and where to display your bonsai is up to you, but the silhouettes of your trees will look better set against a plain background.

You may choose to display them outside.

Reed matting and bamboo fencing make an excellent backdrop, as does your greenhouse. Paint the glass white to give a plain backdrop.

Look around for garden ornaments so that your bonsai landscape is always evolving. You will find a wide selection of bamboo fountains, garden benches, bridges, iron lanterns and Buddha statues to choose from.

As your bonsai knowledge and enthusiasm grows, so will your landscape.

 Do it the Japanese way by positioning your bonsai outside in slatted gazebos.

Crafting a Jin

You will come across bonsai trees that have the added interest of patches of deadwood on the branches or trunk. This special ageing effect mirrors the harsh natural conditions of sun bleaching and harsh climactic conditions that become etched on trunks of old conifers living in mountainous regions.

If you want to make your bonsai look gnarled and old you need to know how to create 'jins' and 'sharis'. 'Jins' are the artificial deadwood areas created on branches, 'sharis' the artificial deadwood created on the trunk.

You will need:
- a jin brush
- a modelling knife or a scalpel
- dilute citric acid

In Japan, jins are only acceptable on conifers.

What you do

- Cut through the bark at the base of the branch and cut along the length.

- Peel away the bark and rub down with jin brush to polish it well.

- Treat with citric acid to bleach the wood and make it look seasoned.

Making a Shari

To create a natural looking area of deadwood on your trunk, use the lines of the trunk as your guide so that your shari is sympathetic to the tree. Remember that the bark is not a living part of the tree but a protective covering so careful cutting should not harm your tree.

You will need:
- a sharp modelling knife or scalpel
- a shari chisel known more generally as a jin chisel to indent the wood and gouge it out
- dilute citric acid

What you do
- Cut through the bark firmly so that you make a clean cut.

- Cut again inside the first cut, holding your knife at an angle so that the two cuts meet and the bark between them can be easily peeled away.

- Wet the wood which is exposed.

- Treat with citric acid to bleach the wood and give the ageing effect.

 This is an advanced technique and can go wrong. It should only be carried out on conifers.

121

Tips for Winter and Spring

Winter

- During the winter your bonsai is dormant so there is no need to feed it.

- Protect the root ball from frost by wrapping the pot and the root ball in jute sacking to insulate it against freezing temperatures.

- Keep watering to a minimum – this prevents a moist root ball from freezing.

- Root prune from leaf fall to bud break.

Spring

- Replant your tree in early spring.

- Keep soil moist.

- Protect against night frosts.

- Only fertilise when the growing period has begun or it will lead to excessive growth too early.

- Ideally prune for form before the tree starts growing.

- Stem and leaf prune as necessary through the growing season.

Tips for Summer and Autumn

Summer

- Inspect your plants regularly to keep on top of pinching and trimming.

- Do not let your tree get too thirsty! Water several times a day and add a covering of moss to keep the base cool.

- Keep your tree in dappled shade to ensure against dehydration.

- Be vigilant against pests and diseases that thrive in hot, humid weather.

- Stem and leaf prune as necessary through the growing season.

Autumn

- The shoots have stopped growing so regular pruning is no longer necessary.

- Use fertiliser to boost the life source of your plant during the coming winter months.

- Stem and leaf prune as necessary through the growing season.

- Shape and form your tree.

Bonsai Kit

This boxed set comes complete with the following to get you started:

Bonsai pot – you can complement this with your bonsai tree.

Chinese house – an example of the variety of ornaments available.

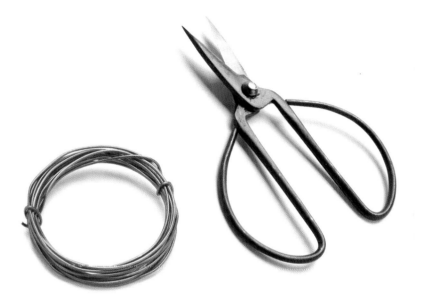

Bonsai wire – to help you train your tree.

Bonsai clippers – build up your bonsai tool kit gradually. Specialist tools can be expensive.

Credits

The publishers would like to thank the following for their contributions to the production of this book:

Consultant Editor – Jonathan Simpson

Groveland Garden Center, Thorpe Market Road, Roughton, Norfolk, UK

www.bonsai-trees.co.uk